The Christian
Book of Questions

THOROLD PUBLIC LIBRARY

RECEIVED AUG 1 6 2003

248 Bos

Boswell, L.
The Christian book of
questions.

PRICE: $9.57 (3797/   )

The Christian Book of Questions

350 Questions to Explore Your Beliefs and Deepen Your Faith

Laura Boswell

THREE RIVERS PRESS
NEW YORK

Copyright © 2003 by Random House, Inc.

All rights reserved. No part of this book may be reproduced or transmitted in any form or by any means, electronic or mechanical, including photocopying, recording, or by any information storage and retrieval system, without permission in writing from the publisher.

Published by Three Rivers Press, New York, New York.
Member of the Crown Publishing Group, a division of Random House, Inc.
www.randomhouse.com

THREE RIVERS PRESS and the Tugboat design are registered trademarks of Random House, Inc.

Printed in the United States of America

Library of Congress Cataloging-in-Publication Data
Boswell, Laura.
   The Christian book of questions : 350 questions to explore your beliefs and deepen your faith / Laura Boswell.
     p.   cm.
     1. Christianity—Miscellanea. I. Title.
BR121.3 .B67   2003
230—dc21   2003005380

ISBN 0-7615-1173-3

10 9 8 7 6 5 4 3 2 1

First Edition

*To every friend and family member of whom
I have asked these questions, long before this
book was written*

Acknowledgments

Special thanks to everyone who assisted in forming these questions—and some pretty good answers, too. Amy, Rob, and Scott, your help was tremendous. Mom, whenever I have asked you one of these questions, you have never failed at least to provide *your* answer. And of course my wonderful mentor and friend, Jennifer Basye Sander—I would not be where I am today without your ever-positive, why-not, go-for-it encouragement. Thank you.

Introduction

I am relieved that this is the *Christian Book of Questions* and not *Answers*. Questions are easy—it's the answers, if they exist at all, that are tough.

Yet despite all this, somehow we Christians strive on. As do Jews, Muslims, Buddhists, Hindus, and those of the countless other religions in this world. We all have our histories, our tragedies, our miracles. No matter what we name our "God," (or "gods") we all wonder why we are here? Why now? What next? This may be a "Christian" book of questions, but these are universal, human questions that almost anyone could ask.

This book came about from years of questions I had tugging at the back of my mind, or questions my non-Christian friends would ask me, for which I had no answers. Sure, I could give a routine rambling about faith or joy, quote a Bible verse or two, and go on my way feeling very proud of myself. But the fact was, I hadn't really helped them at all because I had not given enough thought to what they were asking. I owe it to them, to myself, and even to God, to do so.

I believe God gave us brains and intellect for a reason. If we blindly accept everything we are ever told and do not question it, we do God no good. And in today's society, we face moral and ethical choices never presented before in human history. Should we ignore them? Can we? Or should we, as I believe, use the tools God has given us, in addition to his guidance through prayer and the Bible, simply to figure out the solution as best we can and go on, knowing that he loves us no matter what.

This book has more than 350 questions, some that apply to people of all ages, some more to adults, some more to Christians, some to all faiths. In no way is the presentation or tone of any of these questions intended to judge or promote a particular answer. Again, if I had the answers, this would be a very different book altogether.

I encourage you to read through these questions one at a time or all together, alone or with your spouse, your kids, your Bible study class, or your youth group. I hope that there will be many possible answers presented, and that all are given their fair consideration.

The Christian Book of Questions

Why do you believe in God?

Why do so many people reject the notion of God
but readily accept "Fate" or a "Higher Power"
to guide their lives?

What do you think God looks like?
Why do you think of him that way?

A homeless person asks you for money, but you need
it to buy gas for the ride home. What do you do?

In the Old Testament, God often reacts to sin with harsh, even brutal punishment; yet in the New Testament, he seems more patient and loving even with the most brazen of sinners. Why is this so?

How much should Santa Claus (or the Easter Bunny) be part of your holiday celebrations, if at all?

Many people make bold promises to God in
exchange for help out of tight situations.
Is it necessary to barter with God? Can it work?
What if you break your promise?

If God would answer one question for you,
what would you ask?

Why does God seem to rarely respond directly
to our requests in life? Or does he respond
but we don't recognize it?

On a scale from 1 (completely uninvolved)
to 10 (totally orchestrating everything),
what level of control do you think God has
over your life? Over the world?

Did God *need* to rest on the seventh day,
or did he simply choose to do so?

Can you watch secular TV or listen to secular
music and not be influenced at all, simply
enjoying its entertainment? If you enjoy it,
are you still a good Christian?

Why does God want us to sacrifice our "first fruits"?

Jesus said, "Where two or more of you are gathered together, I am with you also." But what if you are by yourself—does Jesus not come?

Who or what do you think God is most ashamed of in this world right now? What about in the past?

Many Christians believe that God is omniscient—
that he knows everything that has happened
and ever will. If so, why does he not change
things for the better?

Is it possible for God not to know something? Can
he use his omniscience *not* to know something?

Throughout the Bible, and particularly the Old Testament, God often spoke audibly to people and even had lengthy conversations with them. Why does it seem God does not speak audibly to us anymore?

How old is God? Does God age?

The Book of Revelations says our world will end someday. But are we causing it to end more quickly with our sins?

God made us in his image—is that physically, spiritually, or both?

If you pray for a path and nothing becomes clear, can you be blamed for mistakes that take you off the path? Is there a path?

Is it possible to "screw up" God's plan, or does his plan happen regardless of what you do?

What do you truly want out of life? Are your goals aligned with God's plan? How can you know?

Besides "love," what is the one word that best sums up God for you?

What did God do before he created the Earth and its people?

Where is heaven, and what does it look like? Is it in the sky? The universe? Above us? Around us?

Where is hell, and what does it look like? Why do we think of it as below us? Is it below the surface of the Earth? Below Earth altogether?

You work hard for your money and are
financially secure, but your neighbors next door
are struggling. The husband was recently laid off,
and his wife has cancer but no medical coverage.
Do you offer financial assistance to your neighbors?

You can't afford the latest Kate Spade bag,
but you see them being sold on the street.
The vendor looks like he could use the money,
and your friends would be so impressed by your
fashion sense. As far as you can tell, it is either the
real thing or an exact replica—but for a tenth of
what the real bag costs. Is it OK to buy it?

Why must people endure life on Earth before heaven? Why are we not simply born into the presence of God?

Your 10-year-old son is bullied at school. He wants to fight back, but at Sunday School he has learned to "turn the other cheek." What do you advise him to do?

If some of your relatives and friends go to hell,
can you be happy in heaven without them?

Driving home one night, you pass a group of thugs
beating up a man. You are alone with no cell phone.
What do you do?

Your church calls asking for your help during a bazaar next weekend. You have a tough week ahead and don't have any plans other than to relax. What do you do?

Would you be tortured or die for the sake of your Christianity?

You have agreed to sing a solo in the choir's annual concert. Your husband's firm just awarded him a trip to Hawaii as the year's top salesman, and the flight leaves the same day as your concert. No one can replace you in the choir on such short notice, but this is the second honeymoon you both have always wanted. What do you do?

When asked "If you were stranded on a desert island, what book would you bring?" many people answer "the Bible." What book would you choose to bring along? Would it really be the Bible?

If God told you that you could go to heaven right now, would you leave everything here and go?

You are a PTA volunteer at your child's school and have been asked to help count votes for a class election. One of the contenders is a smart-mouthed kid who has been mean to your child. The other is a "geek," a sweet kid who has few friends, is quiet, and makes good grades. The race is tight, with only a vote separating the candidates. What do you do?

Do those who suffer more on Earth
have a higher place in heaven?

Why did Thomas, and others, doubt Christ's return
after all they had seen him do?

If it were possible to create a pill that made everyone good, would you want to take it? Should people who behave badly be required to take this pill?

If you could ask God to grant you one thing in your life, what would it be?

A disheveled stranger comes to your door
in the middle of the night asking for shelter
from a rainstorm. The Bible says to "practice
hospitality," but you have young children
asleep upstairs. What do you do?

If you could ask God for one guarantee in life, what would it be? Would it be for you, for someone else, or for the world at large?

If it were possible to legally and painlessly sterilize sexually irresponsible men and women, would you support doing so?

If you could live forever as a healthy person and see all the people and ages change, or die and go to heaven, which would you choose?

You are stranded at a truck stop on your way home from a trip. Your credit card is being declined and you have no cash, but you desperately need something to eat. Is it OK to steal a bag of chips? What if you reimbursed the store at a later date?

You find a $100 bill on the sidewalk with no clear owner nearby. What do you do with it?

In olden days, no "work" at all was done on Sundays, including work you might find relaxing now, such as cooking, planting, or repairing things. What constitutes work? Would it be so bad to have a day when you really did *nothing* but rest?

Your mother is very ill, and insurance will not cover her care. You are walking home and find a bag of money. Do you turn it in or use it for your mother?

You've been laid off and you must take on another job to make ends meet. However, your new job requires that you work Sundays. Do you take the job as a blessing from God, or do you uphold the commandment to "remember the Sabbath day and keep it holy"?

Your family has fallen on hard times, but you are managing to make ends meet. Your church has offered discreetly to help you, but you know you can manage on your own, even if it is hard. Do you accept the help and get out of debt, or do you refuse it and continue on your own so that someone else may be helped by the church?

Many people wish they had more time to volunteer but do not. If you are truly burdened with work or family issues, is it OK not to make time to help others?

You are involved in a traffic accident in which the other person is at fault. That person accuses you of causing the accident and lies to the police when they arrive. How do you handle this situation? Do you remain calm and honest, risking that the other person is more convincing, or add your own embellishments to the story to get the officers on your side? After all, you are in the right.

Your best friend wants you to go with him to a strip club for his birthday. Is this OK? Does your being single or married make a difference in going to a place like this?

Your boss wants you to lie to a client about one aspect of a product to make a sale. It's a small glitch that will be corrected soon. Do you go along and lie about it?

Some of your friends are going to a party and want you to come along, but you had planned to attend a church dance. What do you do?

Your kids have a championship soccer game scheduled during church time. Do they miss the game or miss church?

Your pastor is convicted of a violent crime, but is freed on a technicality. Do you forgive your pastor and continue to attend that church? Should your pastor be forgiven or be removed from church duties?

You get a bonus from work at the same time your church has a special need. Do you keep the bonus or give it to the church?

A homeless person asks you for money, but you suspect this person will not spend it wisely. As a Christian, are you obligated to give money or food to every homeless person you encounter?

Who is the one person you most want or need
to forgive, and why haven't you?

A person approaches you for money with a story
about his car being broken down. You know he is
lying. Do you give him money or not?

Jesus said, "the poor you will always have with you." But if everyone made an effort to take care of one suffering person in the world (outside your own family), could we eradicate poverty and hunger?

Your pastor commits a *nonviolent* crime but is freed after making monetary restitution. Do you forgive your pastor and continue to attend that church? Should he or she be removed? Must we forgive our pastors no matter what?

Can a Christian be wealthy?
If you are wealthy, are you expected to be more
generous than the average person? What is
"wealth" in the eyes of God?

Is gambling bad if you give the winnings to charity?

If Christmas is supposed to be about peace
and love, why do we get so stressed?

At work, is it Christian to chat on the phone,
punch out early, and take long breaks when
things are slow and there is nothing to do?

Are donations still "charity" if you claim
them on your tax return?

"Tithing" consists of giving 10 percent of your
earnings to the church. Is it all right not to tithe
when money is tight? What would you be willing
to give up so you could continue to tithe?

As Christians, we are expected to forgive, but in today's society, litigation is a common practice. Is it OK for Christians to sue? Is suing simply getting the financial restitution you deserve, or is it more rooted in revenge and punishment?

You have a safe, separate spare bedroom you rarely use. Should you offer it to a homeless person?

Is it OK or wasteful to "upgrade" your tapes to CDs, your VCR to a DVD player, and so on? Where do you draw the line on which gadgets are necessary and which are frivolous? Is upgrading a form of greed?

Why do we struggle so much with tithing when God directly demands it in the Bible? Why does it make us so uncomfortable, considering that these funds are what directly run and grow the church?

Who is the most "Christian" person you know?

Is it wrong in God's eyes to let yourself get out of shape? What is the difference between taking care of your body, your "temple," and vanity?

What would you give to have all the answers? If God gave you all the answers, what would you do with them? Who would you tell?

If you could quit one sin in your life,
what would it be?

Would you endure crucifixion to save the world?

You discover Jesus is coming to take his believers
to heaven in one hour. What do you do?

Have you forgiven everyone who has ever hurt you?
Why or why not?

If you were allowed 24 hours to engage in
the sin of greed, laziness, sex, or gluttony
as much as you liked and with no punishment,
how would you spend your day?

If you could correct the repercussions of one mistake
or sin in your life, what would it be?

A quick, pain-free death is one thing, but would you sacrifice something else valuable—sex, your health, money—for the *rest of your life* to help someone else?
What if that person never knew what you did?
What if they did know yet did not show gratitude?

If you were given the means to start a type of
ministry—a church, a band, a homeless shelter,
or the like—what would you do?

Who is one person you need forgiveness
from, and why haven't you received it?
Did you ask for forgiveness?

In your community, the best school is a religious private school. If you are not of that religion or are not religious at all, is it OK to enroll your children in that school anyway?

If you could live in the time of Jesus, would you give up your life now to have a chance to meet him?

Are you 100 percent sure you are a Christian? Why? Would other people agree?

A healthy and financially well-off Christian woman
desires to have a child, but she is not married.
Feeling that time is running out, she considers
in-vitro fertilization from an anonymous donor.
She would make a very good mother, but is it
wrong for single Christians to "create" children
outside of the traditional family unit?

Why did Jesus speak in parables rather
than in a more direct manner?

Are you 100 percent sure you are going to
heaven when you die? Why or why not?

The Bible says to "be fruitful and multiply."
If a couple has little or no desire to have children,
are they still obligated to start a family?

If you could convince one person of
God's existence, who would it be?

It is difficult to find political candidates today who meet all of our qualifications. Is it better not to vote if you cannot find a candidate who supports your views?

Should you make your kids go to church if they don't want to? At what age will you let your children decide their religious beliefs for themselves?

Why are you a Christian?
When did you become one?

Do angels exist? Do they have wings and harps, or can an angel be the person sitting next to you?

How would you react if your spouse or child killed someone? Would you forgive him or her? What if the person who was hurt was another member of your family?

Your teenage daughter is a rebel and has been in and out of trouble for years. Lately, she has become violent and is stealing from you. She has not shown you love or respect since she was a little girl. What do you do? Forgive her? Kick her out?

Why do so many non-Christians seem
to have great marriages and happy lives in general?
Is God blessing them anyway, or are
they just lucky?

Is it up to you to "force" Christianity
on the children of those who do not believe?
How do you know your beliefs
are good for them?

Why didn't God make it physically impossible
to have babies out of wedlock? If he did,
what would the world be like?

Although God created Adam and Eve for each other alone, eventually in biblical times men took multiple wives or maidservants to produce offspring. Widows could even be "given" to their late husband's brothers. What *are* God's designs for marriage and family in modern times?

If abortion prevents an individual
who would grow up to be the next Hitler
from being born, is that act wrong?

How much should you devote yourself to
your children? Does the importance of your
own life decline once you have children?

What should your children's discipline entail?
Is it wrong to spank them?

Should you marry if you and your partner
have a child out of wedlock?

Your teenage daughter is crazy about a
classmate who is gentlemanly, polite, handsome,
and smart, but he is a professed atheist.
Do you allow her to date him?

In Proverbs, the "Wife of Noble Character" certainly did her share of work: cleaning, raising children, cooking, and spinning flax. But her work was mostly inside the home. Is it "Christian" for women to work outside the home?

If our bodies are made to procreate, why do some people shun parenthood or even abandon or otherwise hurt their children?

A Christian couple desperately desires to have children. After years of trying, they have multiple embryos implanted, resulting in several children—although one dies from ill health. Is this kind of technology part of God's will? Or should this couple have accepted their childlessness?

After the Fall in Eden, was Adam placed to
rule over Eve as a punishment or because
God meant all women to be inferior to all men?
If Adam and Eve were originally created to be equals,
why would having one gender superior to the other
now be considered a good and right thing?
Were they created as equals?

Are women expected by God to be the primary caregivers for children? If the woman works and the father stays home with the kids, is this acceptable in God's eyes?

If parents are atheists and raise their children to be the same, how accountable are those children for their beliefs?

Is it OK for single adults or gay couples to adopt kids even though they might not constitute "traditional" parents?

You and your fiancée are of different religions. What religious teachings will you provide for your children?

What did Jesus look like? We generally think of Jesus as a white man with long hair and a beard, but why?

If Jesus experienced everything ordinary people do, did he feel sexual attraction to women? Why did he not marry and have children before he died, to truly have every human experience?

If you could clone Jesus from DNA found in
his tomb, would you bring him back?

Why did Jesus choose only men to be his disciples but
at his resurrection first reveal himself to women?

On the cross, when Jesus cried out "My God,
why have you forsaken me?" did he sin?

Can genetic testing of unborn children for various diseases be conducted within the Christian context? What if the doctors discover something is badly wrong with the fetus?

Why did Jesus consider the Sadducees and Pharisees evil? Weren't they just trying to uphold their religion as they knew it?

Why would anyone, then or now, believe in
Jesus if they had not seen him in person?
Couldn't he simply have been another false prophet?
How can you believe in someone you have
only read and heard about?

When one woman touched the hem of his garment,
Jesus felt power go out of him. Did this mean
he could become weaker, that people could actually
drain him of his God-given power?

If you took the Bible literally, gave everything away,
waited, and prayed, what do you think would happen?

Was Jesus perfect? Did he ever make a mistake?

Is it better to marry someone of a different religion
or someone with no religious beliefs at all?

There is a promotion you really deserve,
but your coworker is also up for it. In your
interview, you could let it slip that this coworker
used the copier to make copies of a flyer
for his yard sale. What do you do?

Do you think it's OK to sell a product or work
for a company that is not Christian
if it supports you and your family?

Are all your talents gifts from God, or did
you cultivate your talents simply because you
were lucky or worked hard?

If you use your talents for your own glory and not directly for the glory of God, does it bother him, or is he simply happy for you?

Is it acceptable to make a lot of money using talents God gave you? How do you know what to use your gifts for? What do you do with the money?

We are commanded by Jesus to help the needy, yet few of us have jobs that actually make the world a better place. Should we seek work that directly helps those less fortunate?

You seem to have a natural gift for painting, but you use it to paint pictures that some people find offensive. Is this OK to do with a gift God has given you?

Is the Bible the same now as when it was
written, or have changes and errors occurred
in it throughout the years?

The Bible says to ask for things "with prayer and
petition." Should you keep pushing for something
when it appears that you are not going to get it?

In Genesis, Adam was created but did not "live" until God breathed the "breath of life" into him. However, Psalm 139 speaks of how God knit the writer together in his mother's womb. How do we know the starting point of life when verses like these seem to contradict one another?

The Bible says, "Thou shalt not kill." Should you defend yourself to survive and further your religion or be passive so as to set an example by your death?

Is it wrong to tell people you have a negative opinion of them if it helps them, or is that "worrying about a splinter in someone's eye when you have a log in your own"?

Is it important to study the entire Bible, or does just the New Testament matter?

Many of us probably know more lyrics to popular songs than the words of Bible verses. Why don't we know the Bible better?

Can you name all 12 disciples?

We don't know much about Jesus before he was
approximately 12 years old. Would he have been
a normal little boy, or smarter and better behaved?
Did he play? Have friends?

The Bible tells us not to worry and not to be afraid.
Why do we continue to worry and be fearful?

Why hasn't Jesus come back yet?

The Bible says we can move mountains if we have faith as small as a mustard seed, but no one has ever moved a mountain. Is this because our faith is not strong enough, or was Jesus speaking figuratively?

We are told by Paul to "practice hospitality," but what
if company arrives when you are legitimately busy?

In the Old Testament people
lived to be hundreds of years old.
Why is our life span shorter today?

How literally should we take biblical stories?
For example, did Noah really gather two
of every animal? What about bugs?
How could he tell their gender anyway?

It is said that with God nothing is impossible. But is
this really true? Surely we can't get everything we
want in life. What does "impossible" mean?

Jesus says, "Ask anything in my name and
I will do it." If you have tried this, you probably
found it doesn't work—or at least not in the
way you thought it would. Why?

We are taught to turn the other cheek. How do
you make the distinction between "turning
the other cheek" and self-defense?

Is it all right to work on a Sunday if you are in a round-the-clock profession such as health care or law enforcement?

We are told in the Bible not to swear to anything. Should Christians take oaths in court?

Is it wrong for Christians to celebrate Halloween?

Why is Easter not as popular as Christmas?

Is the devil responsible for evil,
or are our sins our own fault?

Do psychics exist?
Can psychic power be a gift from God?

The *Harry Potter* books, with their wizards, witches, and spells, have been used to teach reading in some schools. Are books like these a harmless, fun way to get children to read, or do they popularize the occult?

Is there life on other planets? If God created Earth, might he have created other creatures on other planets, too? How can we know for sure?

Do you believe in ghosts? Is there a place for ghosts in Christianity?

Jesus was crucified by evil people so we would have salvation. Is evil necessary to God's plan?

Is there a devil, or is he just a collection
of stories to scare people into being good?

Are horoscopes just good clean fun?
If they don't predict the future, why do we
bother reading them? Can you believe in your
horoscope and still be a Christian?

The Bible strictly prohibits "sorcery," and it does not deny it exists. Wicca is the religion practiced by self-proclaimed modern day "witches," although their beliefs center more around nature than cauldrons and broomsticks. Do real witches exist? Are they good or evil?

If New Age ideas, crystals, and mysticism help people reach peace and a higher power, are these symbols bad? Un-Christian?

How politically correct are you about other religions and belief systems? Is there a point when political correctness becomes a detriment to Christianity?

The world has many names for the concept
of a higher power: Yahweh, Jehovah, I AM, Allah,
and Buddha to name a few. Ultimately, are we
really talking about the same being?

Muslims pray five times a day. Why do Christians not pray more often and regularly?

Your best Christian friend is getting married and has decided to convert to Islam. Do you support her decision or try to convince her otherwise?

Do children born into other religions go to hell?

How should a Christian dress? Most of us like to wear stylish clothes, but at what point does clothing become too revealing, too tight, or simply too expensive?

Is Jesus the only way to heaven? If someone practiced another religion faithfully, would that person go to hell for not accepting Christianity?

Should Christians undertake modern-day Crusades?
Why aren't we more militant about converting
the world to Christianity if the Bible tells us to
preach the Gospel to all the nations?

If a Jewish person follows the Ten Commandments
and believes in God, but not in Jesus,
will she go to heaven?

Should we teach other religions to our kids in
school? How much do they need to know?

Is it OK to teach kids yoga, a practice
with Eastern religious roots, in school?

When people of other religions or sects try to convert
you, do you turn them away or argue your beliefs?
Is it your Christian duty to try to convert *them*?

Is it possible that there are other books
of the Bible? Are the ones we have
the absolute word of God?
How do we know for sure?

Can New Age charms, crystals, and other symbols truly have healing powers or do they simply provide a psychological crutch?

Is there such a thing as "meant to be"? Does God have in mind one woman for every man? Or do we make someone "meant to be" by working hard or reading signs into what we see?

Does God destine some people to be single?

Are interracial relationships wrong?

Is it OK to join a Christian singles Web site,
or is this interfering with God's plan for our lives?

Your spouse has been unfaithful. According to the Bible, you are allowed to divorce but are also told to forgive. What do you do?

In romantic relationships, does God care about religious differences? If so, why are we still attracted to those of different religions?

Is homosexuality biological or a choice?

Does "adultery" mean any sex outside of marriage, or sex outside of marriage only once you are married?

There are many committees and volunteer outlets at church. Why don't you participate more in church leadership?

Is sex outside of marriage a sin if you are going to get married anyway?

Why do Christian marriages fail,
just as secular ones do?

Are we living in the end times?

Are terrorist attacks, famines, and natural disasters
predicted in the Bible or just coincidental?

How literal is the Book of Revelation?

If Sunday is a day of rest, why do we have to go to church? What's wrong with watching football—that's rest, right?

Is it acceptable to God for women to be ministers? After all, Jesus only chose men to be his disciples.

There are many different degrees and schools for ministers. How do we know which ministers are truly qualified? Is schooling necessary if their gift comes from God?

Are ministers divinely chosen?

Some contemporary churches have a
casual dress code and play modern music in their
services. Is this acceptable in God's eyes?
Is it possible to stray too far from
God's idea of a "church"?
What *is* his idea of a church?

Some "mega churches" have thousands of members. Can a church ever be too big?

Is it OK to skip church if you spend time instead reading the Bible or watching a TV church service?

Is it wrong to go to churches of different denominations?

Many Christians are lax about supporting
their church. Is it OK to visit various churches
and even give money, rather than joining
and supporting one church?

If your pastor/church agrees with you on most points but not on one major one, do you change churches/denominations?

Should you clap for musical performances in church?

Is it irreverent to have Christian bands play on the altar in church?

Is it wrong to miss church because you have
too much work to do?

Can evolution and Christianity co-exist?
What is a Christian explanation for fossils?

Is it enough to attend church but not participate in Sunday School or Bible study?

Is the peace we feel with God truly peace, or is it a natural, psychological elevation we achieve when we systematically sit still, study, and worship him?

Is it OK for Christians to drive fast cars or SUVs if they don't need them?

How do you know if it is indeed God telling you something or just your own mind or heart speaking?

Is it OK to miss church when you are hung over from drinking the night before?

If life is "a gift" but we could go to hell for
living sinfully, why must we be born and live
at all and face that risk?

If we are supposed to sell all we have and follow Jesus,
why do any of us own anything?

Why do some children, who are innocent and cannot yet understand God or Jesus, suffer?

God says "vengeance is mine," but when does this ever seem to happen?

Is it better to hurt someone's feelings or tell a white lie?

It is so difficult to believe in
someone/something we cannot see, yet that
is a core foundation of being a Christian.
Why does God ask something of us
that for many is so hard?

Do miracles happen, or do they
have scientific explanations?

Do saints exist today?

Does God still appear to people in visions?

If the "fall of man" did not occur, what would
the world be like today? Would we be like
Adam and Eve, naked in a garden of bliss?

In biblical times God often spoke and appeared
to his people (as a cloud or a burning bush,
for example). Why did some disobey him
even after hearing his voice?

Why did God create mosquitoes, fleas, viruses, and other nuisances that seem to have no good purpose?

Why would God allow a creature to go extinct—
or is he allowing *us* to cause its extinction?

If we are made in God's image,
why do we sin so much?

The Bible says we are all sinners. Is there any point in
trying not to sin if we are doomed to fail anyway?

Why do some people "find" God so easily while others
struggle and can't seem to connect with him?

Does the devil, or evil spirit, possess people?

God "delivered" thousands of enemies to David and Moses. What happened to those people and their wives and children? Were they all evil? Did they go to hell?

Do street-corner soapbox preachers spread the word of God, or are they a turnoff for non-Christians?

Could God be a woman?

With whom or what do you think God is the most happy (besides Jesus) in this world?

Does God ever purposely cause pain? Why doesn't God protect Christians from emotional and physical pain? Or does he and we don't acknowledge it?

Is cloning humans a sin?
What if we cloned the best
and brightest Christians?

If God is all-knowing and all-powerful,
why does evil still exist?

If you knowingly repeat the same sins without remorse yet go to church and live an otherwise Christian life, are you truly a Christian?

If you knowingly repeat the same sins but try to repent each time, are you truly a Christian?

Why are love and happiness so difficult to maintain, even for the most devout Christians? Why must we be commanded to love? After all, if you don't "love" grapefruit, you simply don't love it. How much harder it is to love other people?

If you are shy, irritable, or impatient, is this
just your nature? That is, is this the way
God made you, or are these sins? How hard
must you work to change these traits?

Despite the prayers of many people, planes still
crash and people die of accidents and illness.
Why pray at all?

At one crowded village through which Jesus passed, a group of men lowered their paralyzed friend through the roof of a cottage so Jesus could heal him. Can a friend or family member's prayers save or heal someone who does not believe in God?

Does God help and heal even those who
don't believe in him?

If Christmas Day falls on a Sunday, is it OK not to
go to church and stay home with your family?

In Isaiah 1:18, God says, "Come let us reason together." Is it possible to "talk" God into something—to reason with him?

If you believe that God's plan is best, why do you still insist on your own way?

In the Garden of Eden, was Eve solely responsible
for the downfall of Man, or did Adam carry as much
of the burden by accepting the apple?

Does God give bigger challenges
to stronger people?
Does God "give" challenges at all?

Why is "witnessing" so difficult for many of us? Are you afraid to be more outgoing in your witnessing because you don't want to "turn people off"? Is that a valid excuse or just a cop-out?

Is capital punishment acceptable to God?

When we pray for help with something, why does the pain so often linger on anyway?

Jesus tells us that he will carry our burdens for us, yet when we "give" something to him we often continue to worry about it. Why is this?

We are taught the adages "let go and let God"
as well as "God helps those who help themselves."
Which is right?

The Bible repeats the phrase "do not fear" nearly
400 times—yet we fear anyway. Why?
Is it an innate response? Is this a sin?

The Bible says to ask God for anything we
want by prayer and petition and we will receive it.
Is it right to ask God for help in obtaining material
things that others do not have, like houses or cars?

Is it OK for kids' church camps to hold
dances like secular camps do?

Why do some people never seem to
have their prayers answered?

Are the children of rape or incest part of God's plan?

Do animals have souls? Do they go to heaven?

Why would God allow Bethlehem, the birthplace of Jesus, to be in the midst of so much turmoil?

If you kill someone who is evil—a serial killer, for example—are you still committing a sin?

How can we forgive criminals? Are we really supposed to forgive their most heinous crimes?

Is forgiveness meant to help the
other person or ourselves?

We are supposed to go forth and multiply, but
humans are using up our world's resources at an
alarming rate. Will there be too many people one
day? Why would God allow this?

Why do some people seem to get everything
they want while others suffer?

Are people sinners if they commit sins but truly
think they are doing so in God's name, or because
they think he commanded them to?

Can people go to heaven if they truly repent
at the last moment of their lives?

Man was placed over all the animals in the kingdom,
but is it right to fish and hunt for sport alone?

Does God punish us directly, or do we punish
ourselves with the consequences of our own actions?

Is it sinful when non-Christians wear
crosses as jewelry or decoration?

Is it OK to wear expensive fur coats and leather
when perfectly acceptable cheaper alternatives
are available? How much should you spend
to follow styles? Is wearing these types
of clothing abusing the animals God
gave us to care for?

Is it wrong to wear makeup? Is cosmetic surgery
a sin? Why do we try to improve on what
God has given us?

Is it OK for a Christian to appear
on a dating reality show?

Do TV shows reflect society and sinfulness as they really are, or do we act more sinful because of what we see in the media? Should Christians avoid secular books, magazines, and entertainment?

Is it appropriate for actors to thank God at award shows for films they have done that involve sinful scenes?

Some Christian actors believe that by playing sinners they can show the consequences of that lifestyle and therefore work for God in their careers. Can shows with sinful characters or plots be tools God uses to reach his people?

Are actors sinning when their "characters"
have sex outside of marriage, are nude,
or take the Lord's name in vain on a show?

Why does so much of Christian music and TV
programming come across as saccharine and naïve?

The media generally seem to portray Christians as either arrogant or not "with it." Are these images we bring on ourselves, or are they unfair portrayals?

Should you boycott companies that use sexual images to sell their products?

Is it OK to have Christian rock bands?

Athletes often pray in the end zone yet do bad things off the field. Are they really Christians?

Are our government leaders divinely chosen?

We are taught to obey authority, yet what
should you do when faced with corrupt leaders?

Can you safely support a candidate who is against
something you feel is a Christian value if the
candidate supports your other views?

If the police could give out citations for foul language
or rude behavior, would this lead to a better society?

If we are supposed to love one another
and share everything, why don't Christians
live a communal life?

Has the pendulum swung too far the other way
in the United States in restricting school prayer
or the posting of the Ten Commandments?
Can the separation of church and state
overshadow our worship of God?

Two football teams pray to God for help in securing a victory, but both teams can't win. Who does God help? Does he help at all?

The Bible says we are all given talents. How do you know what your talents are? Is it OK not to search for them, or not to use them once you discover them?

Are you uncomfortable discussing your faith
with those who do not share it?

Why is it difficult for some of us to
pray aloud in front of people?

Is it acceptable to modernize Christianity with rap
music and casual Sunday evening worship services to
make it more appealing to a broader audience?

Does God bestow blessings freely, or does he reward
us according to how hard we work for them?

There are many wars in the Bible, but we
are not supposed to kill. Is war ever justified?
Is killing ever justified?

Is a wife required to submit to her husband's will?
What if he demands something unhealthy or unfair?

Does God have a set plan for your life, or does your life flow only according to the choices you make? Do you set your own path and then hope to receive God's blessing?

When faced with a struggle over a parking spot or a place in line at the grocery store, should you always give it to the other person? Is this a kind of Christian giving or a sign of weakness?

If painful childbirths are a punishment for Eve's mistakes in the Garden of Eden, is it permissible for women today to have epidurals during childbirth?

Are obese people born with that predisposition, or are they simply guilty of the sin of gluttony?

Is freezing a body after death in hopes of bringing
it to life again one day permissible?

Are the seriously mentally ill responsible
for their religious salvation?

How far should medical lifesaving technology go
in emergency situations? Would you want
such technology used on yourself?

Is cursing a sin?

We often hear of people near death who see white lights or float above their bodies. Are they seeing heaven, or is it just a reaction to the drugs they are being given? If they are really beginning to enter heaven, how is it that doctors have the power to bring them back?

Can psychics really put us in touch with our
dead friends and relatives? If so, is that a
gift from God, or is it an evil act?

We are supposed to treat our bodies as temples.
Smoking has been found to damage the body—
is smoking a sin?

Jesus often drank wine, yet many Christians believe drinking alcohol is wrong. Why? Is it all right to drink as long as we don't become drunk? Is drunkenness a sin?

If we are God's children and have the joy of Jesus' salvation, why do we struggle so much with self-esteem?

Would a cloned human have a soul? Should cloning be considered just another new technology for procreation?

Is using human genomes for research sinful if it could help cure diseases?

God put man in a position to rule over the Earth, and we use its resources for life and health. Do we also have an obligation to protect the Earth's environment for future generations?

Is animal testing acceptable to God?

Why do some people seem to miraculously
be healed while others are not?

Are the people "healed" on televangelist
shows really healed, just faking,
or only think they are healed?

If the devil is evil, why would some
people choose to worship him?

Are drug users sinners?

Is it fair to ask someone to "get high on life"
when so many struggle to do so?

Is suicide a sin? Why does God not rescue
those in such despair that they would
purposely take their own lives?

Is sleeping in a sin?

If a voice told you it was God and that you should go forth and do a difficult task, would you do it?

How can God have no beginning and no end but simply be "I AM"?

Why did God create people in the first place? Did he need company? Entertainment? Assurance?

Would you give up the most important thing
or desire in your life if God asked you to?

So many children are born unwanted;
is this part of God's plan?

What is the Holy Spirit? What does it look like?

If people of other religions follow those
religions to the best of their abilities,
is that good enough in God's eyes?

How many books of the Bible can you name?

Do you know the history of your
church's denomination?

How can God hear the prayers of
multiple people at the same time?

As some other religions grow in popularity,
is it possible for Christianity to be
forgotten altogether someday?

Why do Christians, and society in general, so
routinely use the phrase "Oh my God" when it is
clearly taking the Lord's name in vain?

How far should you go in pushing a
family member to become a Christian—
isn't their life and soul on the line?

Is homosexuality a sin?

Today there exist churches that don't fully acknowledge God or Jesus, but rather the virtues of being good to one another and at peace with life. Because these are virtues Jesus taught, are these churches still "Christian" anyway? Are they churches at all? Is God pleased with them?

If we are made in God's image, why are some people born physically malformed?

When the president says "God bless America," is he violating the separation of church and state?

Is it acceptable for Christians to own guns?

Why do we find it so hard to believe that God has helped us through a hard situation, even when the evidence is very apparent? Why do we try to reason away God's help, or believe we are not good enough for him to bother helping?

Would God help us more if we more readily
recognized it when he did?

Are some people simply born happier and more
positive, and others born more skeptical and
negative? Or are these choices we make?

Is doing mission work in "fun" destinations—
for example, repairing houses in a Caribbean
country—still true mission work?

Can a Christian take part in "extreme" sports like
bungee jumping or skydiving, or is that taking for
granted the life God gave you?

We are told to love one another as we love ourselves, but how are you supposed to love the guy down the hall who plays loud music at 3:00 A.M., or a woman in Namibia whom you will never meet? Isn't it hard enough to love the people closest to us?

Are lunchtime Bible studies at work acceptable, or improper for an office environment?

Is it OK to display religious symbols on your desk at work?

You are visiting a foreign country and are arrested when you stumble into a pro-Christian protest. Do you deny you are a Christian and go free, or maintain your faith?

Is it necessary to be on one's knees to pray?
Are your prayers answered more quickly if you make
time to pray in solitude on your knees rather than
offering up quick, driving-to-work prayers?

What would you do if you won the lottery?

We have all heard of tragedies where a parent turns his or her back for a mere second, and their child falls or drowns or is hit by a car. How could God allow this to happen—not just the tragedy itself, but the overwhelming guilt that parent must feel?

When we die, is it because our "time" has come,
or is it merely a random date?

There have been many instances of missionaries and
other workers for God being killed while performing
their work. Why might God allow this to happen?

Judas is vilified for having betrayed Jesus,
yet without his actions, our salvation would not
have been secured. Was Judas forgiven?
If he had not turned Jesus in, what would
be different for Christianity today?

If women are meant to submit to men's authority, are they still as accountable to God for their sins?

If we are forgiven of our sins via Jesus' death, why do many Christians believe there will be a *"judgment day"*?

In the Ten Commandments, God tells us not to put any other gods before him because he is a "jealous God." What does he mean by this? How can a perfect being have a quality such as jealousy?

We are supposed to thank God for being alive, but life can be so hard at times. Why are we supposed to be thankful for life? If we weren't born, we would never know.

Is downloading your favorite songs off the Internet stealing?

How do you think Mary was treated once people discovered she was supposedly a virgin, but pregnant?

How do you think Joseph reacted when Mary informed him she was pregnant, but he had not been with her?

Does God give us only what we can bear, as the adage says, or are our circumstances only random?

Do we not get what we want because we
lack faith or because what we want is not part
of God's plan? How can we know what to have
faith in, and what to release as God's plan?

Is depression a sin or a condition
that cannot be helped?

In *A Child Called It*, author Dave Pelzer describes his hellish childhood of abuse and torture at the hands of his mother. For years he prayed for release, but with no apparent action from God. Why would God (seemingly) not answer the prayers of a desperate child?

Is speeding a sin?

The Bible tells Christians to "love thy neighbor"
but also to be "equally yoked" in our relationships.
Should we only select Christian friends?

Is borrowing something without asking a sin?
What if you plan to return it immediately?

Did God create different races, or are they a
product of evolution? If we are all God's children,
why is there so much racial disharmony?